To Dance in Stardust

Written and illustrated by Shelby Marie

Also by Shelby Marie

To Walk on Moonbeams

To Matt

———

For unfailingly believing in all of my dreams,
thank you for keeping them alive
on days when I feared
they might have stopped breathing.

Promise me this

if the darkness threatens to consume,
you will set your heart afire,
you will walk on moonbeams
and dance in stardust,
you will burn brighter
than that absence of light.

CONTENTS

STARLESS NIGHTS

I lie near Death
until morning comes,
until I have to say goodbye
to my darkness,
but it leaves me hollow
for Death and I
have grown to be close lovers,
always testing how far
we can push one another,
taking crumbs from plates
with greedy little fingers,
desperate for a taste of forever.

Anxiety.

This is what I have become.
This is who I am.
The diagnosis doesn't
make the feelings subside,
it just brands them on my skin.

I put pressure on myself.
Maybe I'll become a diamond.
Maybe I'll become dust.

These bruised,
under eye circles
are a work of art,
crafted from long nights
spent lying awake,
sinking fingernails into my chest,
trying to pull my beating heart
from beneath lonely moonlight skin,
troubling my thoughts
with useless questions.

How much longer can I hold on?

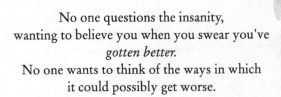

No one questions the insanity,
wanting to believe you when you swear you've
gotten better.
No one wants to think of the ways in which
it could possibly get worse.

I walk
s l o w l y
like sweet molasses,
s t e a d y
so I don't lose my balance,
but anxiety is a storm
and I can't dance on tiptoes
around so many
frantic and frenetic
bolts of lightning.

Why is my mind trying to hurt me?
Why am I letting it?

Teacup rattling again,
I tremble,
cannot still these hands.
I live with Death
always a breath away,
always gazing longingly,
reaching for me.
But I need this,
the way that fear
makes me feel alive.
I want to be wanted,
even if it is something
I may not survive.

I often wondered
how much I could take
before I shattered
into a million
sparkling pieces.

I am more beautiful
than glittering snow.

And I am just as cold.

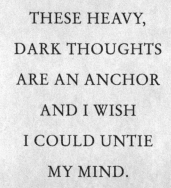

THESE HEAVY,
DARK THOUGHTS
ARE AN ANCHOR
AND I WISH
I COULD UNTIE
MY MIND.

My chest is consumed by wildfire
and my heart believes
there's not enough water
to douse the flames.

- *hopelessness*

It seems the mask I wear
is enough of a distraction
to cover up the sound of my breaking.

I am stuck standing
in the middle of a crowded street,
s c r e a m i n g,
but no one looks my way.

My skin stings
where the sun was too much for it.
It peels back in layers that I cling to.
I can't lose another piece of myself.
What would I have left?

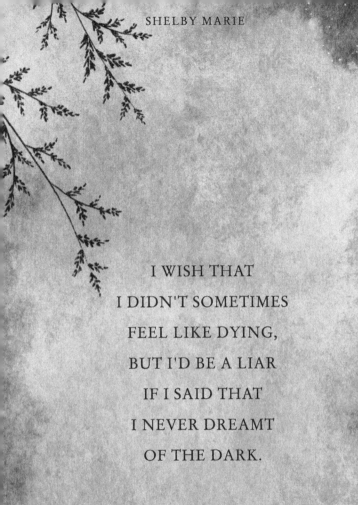

I WISH THAT
I DIDN'T SOMETIMES
FEEL LIKE DYING,
BUT I'D BE A LIAR
IF I SAID THAT
I NEVER DREAMT
OF THE DARK.

THE SUN
WON'T WAKE UP

This heart of mine
is so tired.
I can hardly fathom
why it would choose
to keep beating.

I wonder if the earth forms cliffs
without the safety of water
waiting at the bottom
so we can rest knowing
that if our pain ever
becomes too great,
we still have a way out,
just in case.

I am not afraid
of endings,
of death or the fog.
I have spent a lifetime
gazing upon the reaper,
braving the abyss.
I do not rush towards it,
nor do I race from it either.

Nothing stops
and the world goes on,

even though,
         even though,
                 even though.

I hate that I still need these words.
Maybe I'll burn them,
toss these lines into the fire
and watch them ignite,
watch the letters curl into themselves
and disappear.

Sometimes I wish I could be a sentence,
so easily erased and rewritten.

And yet, I'm still not ready
to be confined in a cage,
worry what the world might do
once it uncovers this sickness.

Everyone says they want to live,
but no one is brave enough to admit
that at some point,
they've wished that they could die.

And I'm stuck,
so I write the words
I'm too afraid to say aloud.

*I am alive
and sometimes I want to die,
but more than anything,
I want a reason to live.*

If the wounds you tend to
are self-inflicted,
does that still count
as taking care of yourself?

The siren is calling me to the sea,
singing sweet melodies
meant to ensnare and lure this body
towards the deathly crashing waves
where she'll devour what's left of my soul.

But I'm still lingering on the shore,
never quite completely entranced,
for I am not entirely human myself.

My monsters have made a home in me.

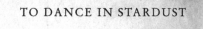

THE THING I'VE COME
TO FEAR THE MOST
IS MY TWISTED MIND
WHEN IT CARES NOT
IF IT SEES TOMORROW.

Too much.
Too much.
Too much.

Not enough.

How can I be both?

I have wished on stars,
told them secrets,
begged them to give me back
all of the reasons
that I ever had to stay.
But they don't know
where I've misplaced them.

I can't find my reasons.
I can't find my reasons.

Anxiety tells me
it is safer on the ground
so I keep my head down,
stop looking to the sky.

I forget the taste of morning sunshine,
the chill of early winter winds,
and when I no longer remember,
the darkness creeps in.

Anxiety says it's for the best
and depression clips my wings.

If I am a sunrise, I am one vacant of colour.

If I am a valley, I am one that runs too long.

If I am an ocean, my waves are far too rough.

If I am a heart, I am one that loves too much.

I worried that the haze
might consume me,
that I might lose
what little I had left of myself,
but you looked at me and saw a spark.
You saw past the haunted husk
I'd let this body become,
you saw past the decay
and it stirred up stardust in me,
it unsettled forgiveness,
it gave me a reason to stay awake,
to wonder what would happen
if tomorrow never came.

SATELLITES AREN'T
SHOOTING STARS

I drink my coffee
as black as night,
as raven feathers,
as starless skies,
and you are not afraid
of the shadows I cast.
You approach with a darkness
all your own
and my heartbeat quickens,
my monsters dance.

YOU SAY MY NAME
AND FALLEN STARS
CLIMB BACK
INTO THE SKY.

We are lying in the dark
and my sight has adjusted.
I can see without the light
and I am content to watch you think,
to stare at the crease between your brows,
your eyes dancing around the room
and landing on everything and nothing.

Your slightly parted lips,
god, I want to kiss them,
and I want to be wrapped up
in your thoughts with you.

I want you to take me
away from this place,
to drift into dreams that play
behind your lakeside eyes
while they're closed and still.

I want to sail on a boat,
mar the mirror of the water's surface.

I want to drown in this.
I want to drown in you.

Tell me how you survive
and I'll drink your words
so I might too.

I grow weary in the chaos
that comes after dusk.

I seek refuge in
your warm embrace.

You quiet my monsters,
muffle their screams,
sing me softly to sleep.

The wind has discovered
ways to defy gravity
and I hope to learn that resilience,
to fight against death
as it races for us,
if only so we might have
a little more time.

You say to me

"What has this vicious world
done to you, wild one,
for you to gaze upon death
and think it a gift?"

I admit

"I could write you an endless list."

You promise

"If you do,
I will help you erase every worry,
line by line."

You taste of ancient sunshine,
towering mountains
and unrelenting rain.

You hold me and it feels like
forever could exist
in a single time-stopping second.

You look at me
and my heart knows peace.

The bats are swooping and diving overhead,
dark silhouettes against an infinitely darker night,
but their presence doesn't make me shiver.

You always found more to love
in their midnight flights
than in the morning songs of birds.

I am in awe of the way you find beauty
in the bleakest evenings,
in the way you always search for magic
in what the rest of the world
will only ever see as ordinary.

I have so much guilt.

I'm sorry.
   I'm sorry.
      I'm sorry.

I couldn't eat all of the leftovers,
they're rotting in the garbage.
I didn't reply to your message right away.
You felt obligated to give me
something on my birthday.
Every kindness turns into a burden
right before my eyes.
I've never been able to accept
gifts and grace without feeling
the sadness that's always buried inside.
I am guilty of taking more than I need,
believing I'll never deserve it,
too lonely to give it up,
but how could anyone
hold enough of love?

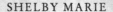

I WONDER IF WE
WILL ALWAYS BE LIKE THIS,
LIKE THE PLANETS IN ORBIT,
LIKE THE WORLD IN
PERFECT BALANCE,
LIKE WE NEED EACH OTHER.

Find me where our horizons meet,
where the sky bleeds red
into the deepest black,
and the sun strains to prolong the day.

Meet me there after midnight,
we'll run together with the moths
and remind them that the light
doesn't always give -
sometimes it takes away,
sometimes it burns.

This night,
it is cold yet inviting,
it is evermore.
Between the stars,
there is a glimmer of hope,
there is a flash of forever.

So I'm not going to blink
if you won't too,
and we'll stay like this,
together,
for however long
our forever might be.

You are sweet
like honey
and warm
like whiskey straight.

11:11,
shooting stars,
dandelion fluff,
four leaf clovers,
I always wish for
the same damn thing:

that our goodbye
will never find us.

I take your hand
and it's warm
like I imagine
the summertime sun
might be.

My heart is
dusted in snowflakes
that never stop tumbling.
It knows nothing aside from
endless winter.

When you reach for me,
I feel the fortress of ice
beginning to melt.

And I believe that
this is what love
is meant to feel like.

I believe that love
is always merciful,
that it always endeavours
to set us free.

DAYLIGHT'S GIVEN UP ON US

You love watching the lightning flash,
and I love listening to the sound of the rain.

We both love the storm, but not in the same way.

Dust dances in sunrays.
The hush of nightfall coats the day.
I sleepwalk, stay close to dreams,
the places where sadness cannot reach,
where loving me seems easy.

If yours is a kiss of death
then colour me crimson
and dig me a grave.

It feels wrong
to burden you with my problems,
my worries,
the thoughts that are screams
clawing at my throat,
drawing blood to escape.
I will not tell you
about any of it
because it's not fair
for both of us to suffer.

Hold me
as though gravity
has lost its grip
on the both of us
and letting go means
we'll drift apart.

I NEVER FEEL
QUITE FULL ENOUGH
OF LOVE
TO KNOW WHEN
IT'S TOO MUCH.

I whispered,
broken and bloody,
lost to the cold,
"I just want to give up."

Trembling hands
wrapped around myself,
a sorry shield,
dented and worn,
and you whispered right back,
defiance sparkling
like crystals catching sunlight
in your worried eyes,
"Don't you dare."

I have always wanted
to save everything
and everyone but myself.
I nurse baby birds back to health
and bring in the strays.
I relocate spiders
when they've gotten lost on their way.
I swerve for squirrels on empty streets,
but I don't know how to turn
that love towards me.
I don't know how to believe
that I deserve it.

Place your palm over this racing heart.
Stop this runaway train of thought.
Stop the surface cracks from splintering.

Stop the beating.
Stop the breaking.
Stop the bleeding.

I wish that I could hold
the sun in my hands,
capture its glow
and let the light in.

How strange it is
to live a long life
with anxiety
and realize that
only I have ever seen
the world in this way.

My eyes are not your eyes.
Your mind is not my mind.

I'll give you
all of the love
I don't think
I'm worthy of myself.

It is too much to hold.

Oh, how the leaves gently sway
with the changing autumn breeze,
how they spin and cascade so wondrously.
To dance before death is to laugh
at the absurdity of it all.

The world isn't supposed to spin like this.
It's not supposed to be off balance.
We tiptoed around the fire so carefully,
how did we get burnt?

Our skin is screaming.
These tired bones, no soaking or resting
is enough to stop the marrow from flaking,
from following the wavelengths of wind
that fuel the wildfire.

The leaves are changing.
The world is dying
and so are we.

So are we.

We could make wishes on dandelions,
but our dreams won't come true
while we're sitting here waiting.
Run, wild heart. Run.

NIGHT RAGES ON

Please,
I'm begging you,
break the ice.
Help me escape this sunless cold.
I miss the feel of oxygen in my lungs.
I want to feel alive again.

I have never been free.
You see, I'm in a constant state of battle,
believing nothing is ever as good as it seems.

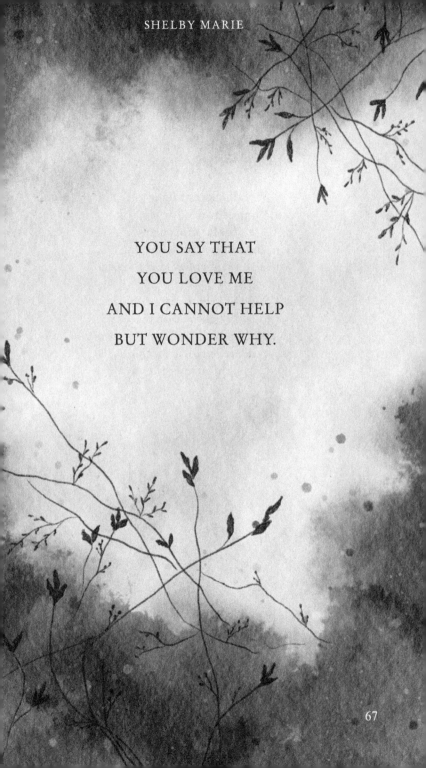

YOU SAY THAT
YOU LOVE ME
AND I CANNOT HELP
BUT WONDER WHY.

You finally turned the heat on
when the first of winter's frost
started to creep along the window's edge.

I'd been shaking
right down to my bones
for far too long,
and I knew you were lying
when you said you were too warm.

Still, I couldn't bear to say anything at all.
I couldn't fight you on this one,
because I could tell just how desperately
you needed to be the thing
that stopped my shivering.

Kiss me
and tell me,
can you taste
my bitterness?

You tame my monsters
so my dreams remain dreams,
are less likely to be nightmares
gnawing at my seams.

But I can see you're growing tired.
I too know how the sword and shield are heavy.

You deserve a fairytale,
a once in a lifetime love.
You deserve the kind of love
you never have to question.

I cannot allow you to stay.

I sometimes wonder
if my time would be better spent
searching for ways to save myself,
rather than tearing
what is already broken apart.

But it seems I cannot help it.
These idle hands make a mess of everything.

Letting you love me
is like putting a bandage
on a cut that needs stitches.

Even if the damage mends miraculously,
we know it'll never heal quite right.

I'm giving up
because the sooner I'm gone,
the sooner you can grieve.

I'm trying to shorten your suffering.

MY NIGHT-DARK

DEMONS

ARE LOUDER

THAN YOUR LOVE.

I DON'T BELIEVE
IN MORNING

Something is wrong.
I feel awake,
but I don't feel alive.

I'm gasping for air,
but there's only
cold, raging water.

I'm drowning
and thrashing,
and I can't find the surface.

I'm reaching for you,
but you're no longer there.

I don't want to miss you,
but my darling,
I do.

I am a haunted house.
The doors all open on creaking hinges.
There are secrets whispered
through these walls,
kept in hidden spaces,
beneath floorboards that are
near to rotting through.
Branches tap on cracked glass windows,
screeching, "Let us in,"
as if this is shelter, as if this body is a home.
There are ghosts that slide down the banister
and rattle the diamond chandelier.
Black cats hiss on the porch,
claws digging in, backs arched, fangs bared.
And I am a banshee,
letting agony escape through
these chapped and bleeding lips,
lace veil tattered,
letting the cold sneak through,
weaving words about all that could have been,
and all that was taken from me.

Snowflakes settled
in a blanket while we danced.
Laughter sounded through empty halls.
I miss the little things more than most.
Your coffee cup used to sit next to mine.

I wish I knew
why I can't let go
of the ghost of you,
why the thought of home
feels hollow if you're not there,
why every wish
that's made upon a star
now feels wasted,
as though I had
everything I'd ever need
and I felt it disappear.

THE DEAD
NEED NOT HAUNT ME
BECAUSE THE LIVING
ALREADY DO.

When they ask why we have broken,
I will tell them that the fault is mine,
that everything I love finds a reason to die
and if I love and lose one more time,
I fear it is something I will not survive.

I have forgotten what it means
to breathe happiness in,
how hope feels when it's held in your hands.

When the world asks why we have splintered,
why we are fragmented, lost and grieving,
I'll tell them it was necessary,
that all that we love must one day leave,
that soulmates are almost never
destined for forever,
and I believed that you were most certainly
never destined for me.

It is easier to move on
when you have someone else
to fill the emptiness.

*But my heart
doesn't have room
to replace you.*

I left my own footprints in the snow,
wondered how long it might be
until I stopped pretending
you were leaving a trail beside me.

His hair was greasy
like the diner we sat in,
but his eyes were
the same colour as yours.

I will do whatever it takes
to carry pieces of you with me
while you're gone.

The trees never got their leaves
and the flowers didn't grow.

It snowed.
It snowed.

Everything remained cold.

I can't find the heat
while you're not next to me.
I no longer feel the sun.

It only ever storms,
the skies are always grey.

When I wake there is grief,
and snow,
and snow.

I have made a home in the darkness,
pulled the moon from the sky,
rearranged constellations,
made the stars spell out your name.

I have sunken shredded knees
into slick, muddy soil,
cursed the heavens for always giving
with the intent to take away.

I am unravelling, slipping into shadows,
the light no longer remembers me.

Watch as I leap above shrouded sea
and realize I've forgotten
that I let them clip my wings.

Watch me fall apart.
Watch me fall.

The day is done
and I am still so numb.

The coming and going
of the brightly shining sun
doesn't always mend
what's been broken.

Sometimes a fresh start
doesn't change anything.

Sometimes the past decides
it'd much rather stay
rooted in the present.

And sometimes our hearts forget
that it often hurts less
if we choose to simply let go.

THE SUN STAYED
WITH THE MOON

We were younger then,
when I sipped love from your lips
like sweet dripping honey.

We were a mirror of the sky,
made of stardust and magic,
wishes and light.

I am sorry
that I let you down,
but I can hardly
hold myself up right now.

Getting better is a process.

The morning sky
is hazy blue,
foggy with hurt and hope,
lost like the stars
that aren't a part
of any constellation.

- *me without you*

I toss and the blankets
tangle uselessly around me.
This bed is too empty.
There's blood everywhere
and I tried a jigsaw to carve
my heart out of my chest in desperation,
but it's still racing,
buried beneath pillows and sheets.
I don't know how to pull the love from it.
I have tried syringes and scissors,
gave up and switched to gentler means,
but nothing will make it give up its memories.
I don't want to miss you,
but even losing the most essential part of me,
is not enough to erase
all that we should have been.

The longer I stare
into the mirror,
the more my reflection
morphs into a monster
and I can't find
what you used to love in me,
but I hope that if I gaze
long enough into the abyss,
perhaps one day I'll see it.

Things I've Thought Lately Because I Was Lonely

1. Grief Lightning is a strange name for a nail polish colour
2. This is too long to hold on
3. Your scent is on my pillow
4. Your heart beats in my chest
5. I can feel you while you're gone
6. It's like you haven't really left
7. The thought doesn't make the pain any softer
8. I wish I'd never pushed you away

I don't want to dream any longer.
I want to feel the heat of your skin,
to taste your kiss lingering on my lips.
I need to hear the rhythm of your heartbeat
while you're pressed up against me.
Distance is a coffin
I can't claw my way out of.

I hope that right now
there are spring flowers
blooming beyond your window.
I hope that beauty and sunlight
follow wherever you go.

*Even if that joy
is something I will never know.*

My dreams are dying.
I am withering too.
I couldn't banish
the ghost of you,
it endures,
like petals pressed
between worn pages,
lasting longer
than I know they should.

Every time I've been
standing on the ledge,
the void beckoning,
it's your voice that I hear
inside my head,
pleading endlessly.

"Wild heart,
please don't feel
you have to do this."

Dawn is smothered
by mist and cold.
Your warmth and glow has faded.
Good things don't last,
but they always come back.
Hope whispers softly
to have patience.

I must keep moving.
If I stop then I will feel
and I'm not ready to face the flood.
I can't remember how to swim.

And I always thought
that it would be so beautiful
to be lost in drowning,
to be weightless,
to see the sun shimmering
just beyond the surface.

But I am not ready to go.
I'm not ready to let everything in
and all I can do is keep running,
keep moving forward
with the dam locked shut,
and remain alive
until I am ready to start living again.

ONE DAY YOU'RE YOUNG
AND LIFE IS SO
ACHINGLY SLOW,
AND THEN IT'S NOT,
AND THEN IT'S GONE.

GLORIOUS
ALPENGLOW

I long to be rid of the monster
that has made a home in me,
so I slice myself open and hope it will bleed out
with the crimson rushing over my skin,
but it doesn't work.

I try screaming at the top of my lungs,
pulling at my hair and closing my eyes
until the world disappears
and I'm sure I won't see that monster anymore,
but it lingers.

And when the pain is too much,
I fall to my knees and let broken sounds escape,
hoping the monster will be washed away
with the ocean of tears running down my cheeks,
but it only holds on tighter.

It crawls behind my rib cage
and it eats my beating heart.

I am losing control.
I am so ready to finally let go.

Someone has to see this.
Someone has to tell me that I am awake,
this is no longer a nightmare,
it is darkness in the day.

Someone has to tell me that
things are going to be all right.
Even if I won't believe it, tell me anyways.

Tell me about your favourite
birdsong in the morning,
how the tangled grass feels beneath bare feet,
how warm the water feels
compared to the chill in the air.

Tell me how to move forward through the day
until I can taste starlight on my tongue
and hear the wind sneak through the trees,
the crickets chirping about some kind of love
I've only ever wished could exist
in a hardened heart like mine.

Someone has to see this.
Someone has to tell me that night gives way to day,
that after dusk there is darkness,
but we'll always find the dawn.

Someone has to tell me that I am awake,
that I'll be okay,
that even though there is darkness in the day,
it never stays.
It never stays.

Are there really angels out there?
Do you think I could get into Heaven
if I really tried?
Do you think, if I changed,
they'd change their minds?

Dearest Death,
won't you dance with me?

Let me show you the way
the stars shine after twilight.
Watch how they spin with us,
how they glow.

Dip me down slowly,
tempt me with your kiss.
Let me taste our ever after
as it drips from your lips.

Dearest Death,
drown me in your eternity.
Bury me in love.

Maybe,
if I started believing in myself,
I'd see that I was wrong,
that my open heart
never made me weak.
It was my softness
that made me strong.

If I must lose control,
help me contain the disaster.
Let the rain that falls
during my storm
drown nothing
and still water the flowers.

If the winds grow rough
and the streets become slick,
pull the people indoors
and give them shelter.

Grant the world its peace
and quiet kindness,
until the worst of my pain
has been washed away
and sorrow seems distant.

If I must lose control,
remind me there is hope
in forgiveness.

I think
what I love most about fall
is that it reminds me
beautiful things might be fleeting.
The colours may fade far too quickly,
the wind might grow raw before we are ready,
but just because it is going to end,
just because we will have to let go,
it doesn't mean we cannot hold on for now.

I see a bird lying on the ground
and its frail bones are broken,
its glazed eyes are lifeless,
and I wonder if it jumped
and spread its wings
because the world said
it was brave enough to fly.

But perhaps it wasn't ready yet.
Maybe it needed a little more time.

If the stars can shine
and survive otherworldly cold,
then I can make it through
these endless arctic evenings,
will close my eyes and dream
the worst is already over,
that good things may still return
from faraway places.

How do we slay
that capricious beast,
silence unflinching anxiety?

S l o w l y.

We conquer it
one fear at a time.

SKIPPING,

HEAVY HEART,

PLEASE BE STILL.

THIS LONGING

WON'T LAST

FOREVER.

I pick at open wounds
so they fester,
absentmindedly.

I curse the heart
that beats in my chest
without notice.

And I let the voices
win the war
sometimes.

But that doesn't mean
I've surrendered.
Perhaps I never will.

I am stuck standing
at the bottom of the mountain,
wings broken from the fall,
but if I give up now,
if I don't keep myself
straightened and strong,
I'll never be so close
to the clouds again.
I'll never brush their
soft smoke plumes
with the tips of my fingers.
I'll never be so close to the sun.

So I'll tuck these splintered
raven wings in tighter,
remind myself that I am stronger
than the battles I've not yet won,
that hope can carry you just as far
as any set of wings can,
that there is more than one way
to make such a climb.

THE CLOUDS
WILL PART

This anxiety wears on me
and most days
it feels like I'm spinning,
but some days
it feels like I'm dancing,
and for those days,
I choose to stay.

I can still believe
the wishes I make
might come true,
that those shooting stars
won't let me down,
that magic exists
for those who need it most.

Not every day
is going to be worthwhile,
not every day will be good,
but I'm beginning to believe
there are still enough days left out there
that will be more than worth the struggle.

If the rain is pouring where you are,
I hope you take this chance
to dance in it
instead of running for cover.

- *small victories*

If Death offered you its hand
and asked if you favoured eternal slumber,
would you reach out and embrace it?

If Life was making promises
you weren't sure it could keep,
would you still put your faith in it?
Would you hope that tomorrow
would be worth waiting for?

Oh, but what if it was Love?
What if Love was standing there instead,
arms spread and grinning wide?
Would that be enough
to make you stay?

It was enough for me.

WHEN THEY BURY ME,

MAKE SURE

THEY LEAVE ROOM

FOR MY DREAMS.

Melancholy settles down to sleep
in these weathered, brittle bones.
I sit, picking at the sand and loam
dried beneath my nails.

The wind seeks my secrets,
the sun weaves gold into my hair.

The world is trying to tell me to stop fiddling,
stop spending so much time in my own head,
to appreciate what surrounds me.

The breeze is soft upon my skin.
It sings a lullaby and ends with a gentle nudge to
look up.

The sunset begs for attention,
paints the horizon in swatches
of rich ruby sparkles
and its signature citrine glow.

When the birds sing,
they remind me that I am home,
that the seasons will come and go
and I will change with them.

I will shiver.
I will grow.
I will bloom.
And when I have lived through
all that I must,
I will learn to let go.

I remember how
you grinned at me,
danced in the fire,
reveled in my flames,
said that when my darkness
reached for me,
I could flee
or I could choose to
burn brighter instead.

I am a moth
with stardust
on my wings.
I find that the light
is always before me.

I've decided to stay
because someone has to tell the leaves
that are curling into themselves,
crumbling and flying away,
that they're beautiful.

Someone has to smile
at strangers on the street.

Someone has to adopt
that last and lonely pet from the store
and show it that the world
isn't as scary as it seems.

Someone has to dance in the rain
and soak up the heat of the sun.

Someone has to let the wind tangle their hair,
catch snowflakes on their tongue.

And it ought to be me.

It really should be me.

I have woven hope
around my bones,
clutched faith
in trembling hands
and leapt off the edge,
no longer afraid of free falling.

My heart has decided
that it feels a hell of a lot better
to be worry-free and weightless.

And because of its bravery
I've remembered why we fight
to stay alive.

I drink the light
of the dying sun.

Ferns and flowers
bloom from my lungs.

I swallow the night hungrily,
spread wings wildly.

*I belong to nothing
but unending dreams.*

There are bluebirds singing
in the tops of swaying trees,
urging blades of green
to break through muddy soil,
asking through melodies
that the crocuses prove
that spring will soon be upon us.
I am lying on the still frozen ground,
watching the clouds pass by
as they're nudged by the breeze,
desperate to witness the flowers,
the season's first bright colours
blooming through the ice,
where the world is still sheathed
in shadow and snow,
waiting to catch a glimpse
of beauty as it rises from ruins.

SUNLIGHT
SHINING THROUGH

Kaleidoscope wings
guide me over
moss and leaves.
I forget the ground
beneath my feet.
I fly,
find fields of wildflowers
and I am alive,
touching sunlight,
chasing the breeze,
tasting tomorrow
like it's meant for me.

The world won't tell you this,
but you don't have to wait
to find out who you're going to be.
I've realized
you can choose.

Because I've learned to love myself,
I no longer know how to dream small.

- bet on yourself

The autumn leaves
are falling,
slowly and with grace,
singing the song
of the season of change.

MAYBE I'M
A LITTLE LOST,
BUT I'M STILL
ON MY WAY.

If the world says
that magic does not exist,
I will still defiantly gaze
up into the night sky
and make wishes
on satellites passing by,
because no one can extinguish
the hope I have
that tomorrow
will bring something better.

I already want
too much from this life.

I could spend an eternity
chasing these dreams.

And my heart,
this wild, reckless thing,
I still hear it when it thinks
I'm not listening,
whispering that somehow
there might be a chance
we could have everything.

NIGHT GIVES WAY
TO DAY

I am alive because you love me,
because you spent your days
showing me there's beauty in the broken.
You pointed out all of the things
that I should love about myself,
and even though my ashen heart
still fights to prove you wrong,
there's a small part of it
that has started to hold on to hope,
that clutches tendrils of faith
and dares not let them go.

I have learned to love myself
and now the night sky seems afire.
I've become its midnight muse.

When I smile,
the heavens sigh,
and shadows spin starlight
into solid gold.

You are not a monster
for letting me push you away.
I was never going to let you save me.

I needed to do that on my own.

You send me postcards
from the places you've been
and even though the pictures always change,
the short messages you write
leave me longing all the same.

*"I hope you'll want to
join me here someday."*

*"These views are breathtaking,
but they're nothing compared to you.
Nothing will ever compare to you."*

*"This place is magic,
and I never would have noticed the signs
if you hadn't shown me where to look for them."*

"I still have hope for us yet."

*"When you're ready,
just know I will come back for you."*

I wake
and the world
feels different.

I write you back
and I wait,
and I wait.

I love you.
I miss you.
If you'll still have me,
come back home.

TOMORROW
DOESN'T MATTER,
NONE OF THIS MATTERS,
WITHOUT YOU.

The stars have fallen asleep
wrapped up with my wishes,
and I am trying to be patient
with those burnt out constellations,
but I miss you.

I am so tired
and I have been for so long,
but love is winding itself towards me,
walking slowly through
the valley paths below.

I want to race down
the side of this mountain
and meet it halfway
so I can hold on a little sooner.

But the wind begs me so softly,
asks me gently
to stay.

So I wait as quietly
as my thundering heart will allow,
and I stay awake
even though I am so worn.

I keep my eyes open the entire time,
afraid to blink and miss sight of
everything I've ever wanted.

And I get to watch as love
walks right up to my door.

I get to see you coming back for me.

If there is magic and hope,
and no longer an absence of you
waiting for me on the other side,
I will walk through.

Even if I have always been
scared of new beginnings,
harbouring hands that tremble
at the thought of change.

And I will close that door behind me,
because you promised me forever,
and I swore it too.

I think that better days
are still on their way,
and I cannot wait any longer
to love you.

Let the touch of my fingers
warm your frozen skin.
Let the constellations spill out.
Let us begin again.

Love is worthwhile
if you're brave enough
and so is forgiveness.

DREAMING WHILE AWAKE

We are no longer
slaves to love,
but still,
we let it in,
we let it in.

It's just you and I
in a world of our making
while we're in love like this,
and no pain nor heartache
can touch us.

We'll be together ever after.

Some say
soulmates don't exist,
but my heart swears
you are the exact piece
it has spent
an entire lifetime
missing.

Do not guide me
out of the dark,
not right away.

I say we sit in the shadows
and provoke our monsters,
unlock their rib cage prison
and set them free.

When they're a frenzy
of claws and teeth,
snapping and snarling,
when they finally look away,
I say we walk together
towards the light
with a little less weight
on our shoulders.

Always.
You'll always have my heart.
Wherever yours wanders,
mine will follow too.

I would go with you
to the ends of this earth,
and past even that
to the places perhaps,
we should be the first
to discover.

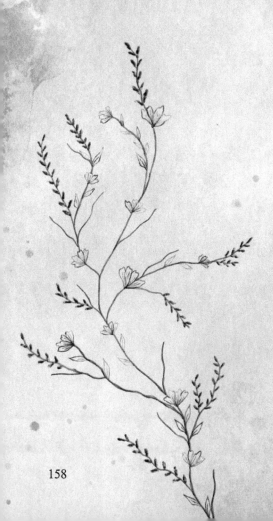

These words,
this heart,
every fragment
of my soul,
it's all for you.

You are a beacon
in the night.
You are home.

"Even after this life ends?"

"Even still."

I might love you
a little too much,
but you deserve
nothing less.

We'll abandon
all our dreams
for just this one,
cast aside our darkness
in favour of the dawn.
We'll surrender our grief
and turn to the sun,
open our hearts
and let in love.

WHAT I ONCE
WISHED AWAY,
I'M GLAD YOU
MADE ME STAY FOR.

The sky is stained
with the papaya sunrise
cresting over the mountaintops,
sweet sunlight licking the wounds
of nighttime before it.

The air is crisp,
the ground dew-kissed
come morning.
And we are dancing,
and spinning, and howling,
and twisting, and letting go.

We are wild in this moment
where everything feels so right,
where our souls are intertwined,
where the darkness
dares not come too close.

For the stars have warned
that absence of light
to keep its distance.

We are uncaged,
holding tight to our keys.

A love like this
might be challenged,
but it'll never be defeated.

We are pure magic,
even if to the world
we don't make sense.

I would stay if there was
even the smallest hope
that you and I
could keep spending time
together like this,
beneath the full moon
and the sparkle of stars,
cheeks reddened with
the caress of wintry wind,
the noise quieted,
peace surrounding us,
reveling in the feeling
that while we have these
midnight adventures,
it feels like
the entire world is sleeping.

WE'LL ALWAYS FIND THE DAWN

To taste the world
in all of its wonder
is such a gift.
I drink my coffee black
and savour the bitterness,
let a spoonful of sugar
melt on my tongue
and dance with the bliss.
In the dry heat of summer,
watermelon drips down my chin.
I warm myself from within
with hot drinks and cinnamon
as the leaves begin to fall.
And when I am truly lucky,
when the stars are
making wishes for me,
you lean in close,
kiss me soft and with promise.
I stand in every season
all at once.
I feel the gates of Heaven opening
and love,
love tastes a lot like magic.

Your touch,
the simple brush
of your hand
against the cold
of my skin,
it's a shock wave
of electricity.
It's perfection.
You're perfection.

Some people
come into our lives
as temporary loves,
but you are not
temporary, love.
You are everlasting.

YOU ARE THE
UNRELENTING SUN,
BRILLIANT,
WARM,
AND NECESSARY.

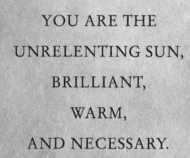

Love is fire dancing at your fingertips,
heating up your edges,
letting embers escape like fireflies
dancing on humid summer nights.

It is getting too close to your flames
and breathing in deeply
despite the smoke clouds rolling,
reaching towards the light
knowing that I will not burn.

Love,
however passionate and out of control,
is always gentle, is always home.

I will greet oblivion
with a full heart
when I settle in my grave,
with love tugging up my lips,
and eternity calling my name.

You smile
and it shatters my faith,
sends me crashing to my knees,
and I have no choice
but to worship
all of the ways
that love is greater
than any god.

Falling stars race autumn leaves,
the moon grins,
we dance with the breeze.
Were this night unending,
I'd still wish for more.
I've wasted so long
tying loss to love.

Like doves,
we were only ever made
for each other.

When I think of intimacy,
I think of you and me
in the dining room
on a slow Sunday morning,
of a polished table
and mismatched chairs.
You cut my hair,
scissors snip at dead ends.
I shed the parts of me
I no longer need,
and you pull the strands
away from my neck,
whisper warmth against my skin.
I ignite like the sun.
Fate is afire.
I become the dawn.
I become the dawn.

I used to love and be afraid
it would run away from me,
fear that happiness would slip
like sand through my fingers,
worry that I would be standing
in the middle of devastation,
alone and wondering
where I went wrong.

I have learned now that love
doesn't bring you to your knees.
Heartbreak does,
loneliness does,
but never love.

Love gives more strength
than it takes away.
Loving you didn't make me weak.
Loving you lifted me up,
gave me life,
gave me a reason to stay.

If I had been so afraid of losing you,
too afraid to let down these walls,
I would have missed out on loving you.

And that has been the greatest adventure of all.

You and I are standing hand in hand,
gazing out at the horizon,
at the sun slowly rising in the morning.

The dewy grass soaks our feet
and the howling wind whispers our secret.
We have gotten better.
We have found the way
back to each other.

We sing a lament for the dead,
for the rotting versions of ourselves
buried behind us in shallow graves.
We raise our voices to drown out
the screaming bones behind us
because we are no longer our darkness.

We are at long last the light.

End

About the Author

Shelby Marie is a poet and small business owner from
Ontario, Canada. When she's not writing poetry,
you'll often find her cozy with a book and snuggled up
with her darling tuxedo cats, Jaximus and Maisie.

Keep in Touch

Instagram: @shelbymarie.poetry
TikTok: @shelbymariepoetry
Facebook Page: Shelby Marie Poetry

Visit the Shop

Check out Shelby's online shop
for more original poetry & handcrafted gifts.
www.shelbymariepoetry.ca

Leave a Review

If you enjoyed reading To Dance in Stardust,
please consider leaving a review
on Amazon and Goodreads.

Thank you for taking such great care
of the paper pieces of my heart.

Much love, Shelby

To Dance in Stardust

Written and illustrated by Shelby Marie.

Made in United States
Orlando, FL
21 September 2024

51766742R20104